PROFESSOR PETER COOPER is Professor of Psychology a[t] Reading and Honorary NHS Consultant Clinical Psychologist. He has worked for many years in the field of eating disorders, specializing in bulimia nervosa and binge-eating. His original book on bulimia nervosa founded the *Overcoming* series in 1993 and continues to help many thousands of people in the USA, the UK and Europe. The aim of the series is to help people with a wide range of common problems and disorders to take control of their own recovery programme using the latest techniques of cognitive behavioural therapy. Each book, with its specially tailored programme, is devised by a practising clinician. Many books in the *Overcoming* series are now recommended by the UK Department of Health under the Books on Prescription scheme. Following a self-help programme is recommended as a possible first step for those suffering from bulimia nervosa by the National Institute for Health and Clinical Excellence (NICE).

Other titles in the *Overcoming* series:

3-part self-help courses

Overcoming Anxiety Self-Help Course
Overcoming Low Self-Esteem Self-Help Course
Overcoming Panic and Agoraphobia Self-Help Course
Overcoming Social Anxiety and Shyness Self-Help Course

Single-volume books

Overcoming Anger and Irritability
Overcoming Anorexia Nervosa
Overcoming Anxiety
Bulimia Nervosa and Binge-Eating
Overcoming Childhood Trauma
Overcoming Chronic Fatigue
Overcoming Chronic Pain
Overcoming Compulsive Gambling
Overcoming Depression
Overcoming Insomnia and Sleep Problems
Overcoming Low Self-Esteem
Overcoming Mood Swings
Overcoming Obsessive Compulsive Disorder
Overcoming Panic
Overcoming Paranoid and Suspicious Thoughts
Overcoming Problem Drinking
Overcoming Relationship Problems
Overcoming Sexual Problems
Overcoming Social Anxiety and Shyness
Overcoming Traumatic Stress
Overcoming Weight Problems
Overcoming Your Child's Fears and Worries
Overcoming Your Smoking Habit

OVERCOMING
BULIMIA AND
BINGE-EATING
SELF-HELP COURSE

A 3-part programme based on
Cognitive Behavioural Techniques

Part One: Understanding Bulimia Nervosa
and Binge-Eating

Peter J. Cooper

ROBINSON
London

Constable & Robinson Ltd
3 The Lanchesters
162 Fulham Palace Road
London W6 9ER
www.overcoming.co.uk

First published in the UK by Robinson,
an imprint of Constable & Robinson Ltd 2007

Important Note
This book is not intended as a substitute for medical advice or treatment.
Any person with a condition requiring medical attention should consult
a qualified medical practitioner or suitable therapist.

ISBN: 978-1-84529-236-2 (PACK ISBN)

ISBN: 978-1-84529-506-6 (PART ONE)

ISBN: 978-1-84529-507-3 (PART TWO)

ISBN: 978-1-84529-508-0 (PART THREE)

Printed and bound in the EU

1 3 5 7 9 10 8 6 4 2

Contents

Note to Practitioners

This self-help course is suitable for a wide range of reading abilities and its step-by-step format makes it ideal for working through alone or under supervision. The course is divided into three workbooks, and each contains a full supply of worksheets and charts to be filled in on the page – so there is no need for photocopying. If you do decide to photocopy this material you will need to seek the permission of the publishers to avoid a breach of copyright law.

Preface

The *Overcoming Bulimia and Binge-Eating Self-Help Course* is an adaptation of my original book *Bulimia Nervosa and Binge-Eating*, published in 1993. This book provided a clear account of the nature of bulimia and its development, and a set of practical strategies for tackling the various components of the problem. Bulimia nervosa continues to affect many thousands of people in Britain and elsewhere, and there is increasing evidence that cognitive behavioural therapy is a highly effective treatment for the condition and its use has become more and more widespread. The original book is recommended widely by clinicians to their patients and has now been updated and converted into this accessible self-help course comprising three easy to use workbooks.

Part One provides an explanation of the nature of bulimia nervosa and binge-eating and an account of how it develops and affects people's lives. Part Two outlines how to monitor what you eat and how to prevent binges. Finally, Part Three explains how to stop dieting once and for all and how to change the way you think about food.

Professor Peter J. Cooper
University of Reading, August 2006

Introduction: How to Use this Workbook

What's in the workbooks?

This self-help course aims to give people with bulimia nervosa and binge-eating problems a way towards recovery. It is divided into three parts.

Part One explains:

- what bulimia nervosa and binge-eating problems are;
- how they affect people;
- what causes them;
- whether and how you might benefit from the self-help course.

Part Two explains:

- how to set about using the self-help course;
- how to monitor what you eat;
- how to plan your eating;
- how to learn to prevent binges.

Part Three explains:

- how to learn problem-solving skills;
- how to stop dieting;
- how to change how you think;

and also contains a section of useful information.

How long will the course take?

It is not possible to say exactly how long it will take you to work through this self-help course. Different people find different parts easier to manage, and most people hit sticky patches where they need to spend longer working on one task or stage. Don't feel under pressure to move on before you are ready. As a rule of thumb, the whole course usually takes three to six months to complete. But you may need longer than this. Take your time, and go at what feels the right pace for you.

How do I use the books?

These workbooks are just that – books for working in. So feel free to write on them! Don't just fill in the question boxes, worksheets and charts, but make notes in the margins, underline things you think are important, or mark things you don't quite understand and want to come back to. We have provided a few extra pages for your thoughts and reflections at the back of each workbook, should you need extra space.

Will it work for me?

The self-help principles presented in Parts Two and Three of this course are based on cognitive behavioural therapy, a well-tested and proven form of psychological therapy that helps you deal with problems in a very practical and personal way. These principles have been used by many people with bulimia nervosa and binge-eating problems to help them towards recovery. It has been shown in recent research that the great majority of people with bulimia nervosa and binge-eating problems also benefit from these principles when they are accessed via the self-help programme outlined below.

How will I know if I've recovered?

It is important to be clear about what 'recovery' from bulimia nervosa means. Many people do recover fully. They find they can eat normally without anxiety and without the concerns about their weight and shape which used to dominate their lives.

However, many people find they still sometimes have difficulties with food and related concerns, even if these problems only surface on rare occasions of stress. If you find that these difficulties still come up from time to time, this does not mean that you have not recovered. Part of a realistic notion of recovery is accepting that difficulties with eating may occasionally come back, but that they can be dealt with using the principles set out in this course.

Using the book to help someone else

- This book is intended mainly for people who have bulimia nervosa or binge-eating problems themselves. However, it will also be helpful to others. The families and friends of people who binge often want to know more about the problem.

- If you are using the course yourself, it may well be helpful if someone else – a parent, partner or friend – knows what you are trying to do so that they can help and support you.

- Finally, it is suggested in the self-help course that the person using it gets someone to help them. This could be a friend or relative, but it is even better if it is someone less close to them, such as a general practitioner, a nurse or a dietitian. This person will need to know what advice is contained in the course if they are to give the most help they can.

A note on gender

Because most people who binge and/or suffer from bulimia nervosa are women, the user of these books is referred to in the text as 'she' and 'her'. This is by no means intended to imply that the course is directed only at women; some men also suffer from these problems, and they are just as likely to benefit from following this programme.

SECTION 1: What Are Binge-Eating and Bulimia Nervosa?

Binge-eating

Almost everyone at some time or other overeats, and lots of people feel a little guilty and ashamed when they do. Such episodes and feelings are very common, perfectly 'normal', and not a source of concern. For others, overeating is a very different experience. They would say, with deep shame and remorse, that they lose control of their eating and 'binge'.

It is not only overweight people who binge. Indeed, about half those with the eating disorder anorexia nervosa, who are by definition very thin, binge-eat from time to time. And some people whose weight is within the normal range also binge. Many of these have an eating disorder which has come to be known as *bulimia nervosa*. As well as binge-eating, these people go to great lengths to make up for overeating and are constantly preoccupied with their body shape and weight.

> *'I began binge-eating when I was about seventeen. I was lonely, shy and lacking in self-esteem. Every binge made me feel worse, made me hate myself more. I punished myself with more and more food. Within months I was binge-eating as a matter of course, and I gained weight rapidly. I loathed myself and only continued with normal life by pretending to be "normal".'*

What is a binge?

The word 'binge' means different things to different people, so it is useful to agree a definition at the outset. Over the past few years those working with eating disorders have come to agree that a true binge is an episode of eating marked by two particular features.

- First, the amount eaten is, by 'normal' standards, excessively large.

- Second, the person feels as if she has lost control.

> *'It starts off with me thinking about the food that I deny myself when I am dieting. This soon changes into a strong desire to eat. First of all it is a relief and a comfort to eat, and I feel quite high. But then I can't stop and I binge. I eat and eat frantically until I am absolutely full. Afterwards I feel so guilty and angry with myself.'*

What is a binge like when it is happening?

Binge-eating is usually done:

- in secret;

- very hurriedly;

- in a feeling of desperation.

> *'I randomly grab whatever food I can and push it into my mouth, sometimes not even chewing it. But then I start feeling guilty and frightened as my stomach begins to ache and my temperature rises. It is only when I feel really ill that I stop eating.'*

Binges almost always take place in private. Indeed, a lot of effort goes into keeping this behaviour secret, often for many years, with an appearance of 'normal' eating being kept up in front of others.

Many binges take place where food supplies are kept, often the kitchen. Some people binge while buying food, eating between shops.

> *'I leave work and go shopping for food. I begin eating before I get home, but it is secret, with the food hidden in my pockets. Once I'm home proper eating begins. I eat until my stomach hurts and I cannot eat any more. It is only at this point that I snap out of my trance and think about what I have done.'*

Usually, the food eaten in a binge is consumed very quickly. It is stuffed into the mouth almost mechanically and barely chewed. The first moments of a binge are often described as pleasurable; but soon all sense of taste and pleasure is lost. Many people drink a lot during binges, which makes them feel even more full and bloated.

> *'When the urge to binge comes I feel hot and clammy. My mind goes blank, and I auto-matically move towards food. I eat really quickly, as if I'm afraid that by eating slowly I will have too much time to think about what I am doing. I eat standing up or walking around. I often eat watching television or reading a magazine. This is all to prevent me from thinking, because thinking would mean facing up to what I am doing.'*

Many people describe their binges as frenetic and desperate affairs. There is a powerful craving for food which they experience as overwhelming. It is this sense of being driven to eat which has led some to use the term 'compulsive eating' to describe binge-eating. The desperation people feel drives them to do things they would never normally do, such as taking food belonging to their friends, stealing from shops, or eating food that others have thrown away.

'I begin by having a bowl of cereal. I eat it really quickly and then immediately have two or three more bowls. By then I know that my control is blown and that I am going to go all the way and binge. I still feel very tense and I desperately search for food. These days this means running around college looking for food people have thrown out. I know that this is really disgusting. I stuff the food down quickly. Sometimes I go into town stopping at shops along the way. I only buy a little from each shop so as not to arouse suspicion. I stop when I have run out of money or, more usually, because I am so full that I physically cannot eat any more.'

What is eaten, and how much?

How much is eaten during a binge varies greatly from one person to another. Occasionally someone will describe regularly having binges of 20,000 calories or more. This is not typical. The average content of a binge tends to be between 1,500 and 3,500 calories.

'After a binge I feel so full that my stomach hurts and I can hardly move. I feel sick and sometimes, when I have had a particularly bad binge, even breathing is difficult and painful.'

Some people have eating episodes which are not binges as defined above but which they nevertheless see as binges because they feel out of control and eat when they would prefer not to. These 'binges' have been called 'subjective binges', to distinguish them from true 'objective binges'.

True binges typically consist of:

- bulk foods which are filling and high in calories;

- foods that people regard as fattening and which they are attempting to exclude from their diet.

Many people believe that binges are especially high in carbohydrates, and that binges are driven by a specific 'carbohydrate craving'. This view is mistaken. Compared to normal meals, binges do, indeed, contain more carbohydrate; but they also contain more fat and more protein. And the proportion of a binge made up of carbohydrates is almost exactly the same as in normal meals.

'The food I eat usually consists of all my "forbidden" foods: chocolate, cake, biscuits, jam, condensed milk, cereal, and improvised sweet food like raw cake mixture. Food that is easy to eat. Food that doesn't need any preparation. I never eat these kinds of food normally because they are so fattening. But when I binge I can't get enough of them.'

What triggers binges?

The things that trigger a binge can be divided broadly into three kinds:

- events or thoughts concerned with food and eating;

- events or thoughts concerned with body shape and weight;

- negative moods or thoughts.

Here are some examples of how this works.

1   An event or thought concerned with food and eating might be:

- breaking a dietary rule;

- having 'dangerous' (i.e. 'fattening') foods available;

- feeling full after eating;

- thinking about food.

'The urge to binge usually begins around midday on a 'normal' day – that is, a day on which I am trying not to eat. During the afternoon thoughts of food become more and more of a preoccupation; and eventually at around 4.00 p.m. my power of concentration will be sufficiently non-existent for thoughts about food to be totally overwhelming. So I leave my work and go to the shop.'

'One thing that definitely sets me off is hunger. If I am hungry, instead of eating something to satisfy it, I eat anything I can lay my hands on. It's almost as if I have to satisfy all tastes, even for things I don't like.'

2   An event or thought concerned with body weight and shape might be:

- brooding about shape or weight;

- discovering weight to be higher than expected;

- feeling fat;

- discovering clothes to be too tight or too small.

'If I discover my weight has gone up, or I find that my clothes are too tight, or I look in the mirror and see that I am too fat, immediately I want to eat. I know this is silly when I really want so desperately to be thin, but I just feel as if I can't cope any more and I might as well just give up and eat. Of course, I feel even worse after the binge.'

3 A negative mood or thought might be:

- feeling miserable or depressed;

- feeling lonely or isolated;

- feeling tense, anxious or fearful;

- feeling angry or irritable.

> *'Binges start when I'm tired or depressed, or just upset. I become tense and panicky and feel very empty. I try to block out the urge to eat but it just grows stronger and stronger. The only way I know to release these feelings is to binge. And binge-eating does numb the upset feelings. It blots out whatever it was that was upsetting me. The trouble is that it is replaced with feeling stuffed and guilty and drained.'*

Think back to a recent binge-eating episode. Write down:
what you were doing before you started eating:

_____

_____

_____

how you were feeling before you started eating:

_____

_____

_____

Do your answers echo any of the triggers identified above?

How does a binge make you feel afterwards?

The emotional feelings people have after binges are a complicated mixture of:

- relief at having given up the struggle not to eat, followed by

- shame, guilt and disgust, and often

- depression and hopelessness about ever being able to control eating, with

- acute fear of gaining weight.

These feelings are made worse by the physical effects of binge-eating:

- feeling extremely full and bloated, along with
- tiredness,
- abdominal pain,
- backache,
- headaches, and
- dizziness.

'After a binge I feel agitated, annoyed and frightened. Fear is a large part of what I feel about my eating, especially when I am totally out of control and horribly alone. My stomach and back ache and I feel hot and panicky. I am terrified about the weight I have gained. I feel full of anger towards myself for allowing it to happen yet again. I feel unclean inside. Dirty. I don't want anyone to see me. I hate myself.'

Think back to a recent binge-eating episode. Write down how you felt after you stopped eating. Take as many or as few words as you like.

_____

_____

_____

_____

_____

_____

How do people compensate for binges?

Many people who binge make great efforts to compensate for their episodes of overeating. As well as strict dieting or even fasting, people may:

- exercise excessively, perhaps for many hours every day;
- take appetite suppressants;
- make themselves vomit and/or take laxatives or diuretics.

This is the basic pattern of bulimia nervosa: binge-eating, then attempting to compensate for it in extreme ways. In fact, as we shall see in this section, these extreme ways of attempting to compensate for binge-eating at best have no effect at all and at worst keep the problem going.

Dieting

Most people who binge are at the same time trying to lose weight by dieting. In fact, they are usually dieting before they start binge-eating. Then, understandably, they go on dieting in response to the binges driven by the fear of putting on weight.

There are basically three ways in which people diet in order to lose weight, and all three are typical of the eating habits of people with bulimia nervosa. These are:

- fasting, that is not eating anything at all for long periods;

- eating only small quantities every day;

- avoiding certain types of food believed to be 'fattening' or to trigger binges – often called 'forbidden', 'bad' or 'dangerous' foods.

The problem with all three of these methods of dieting is that they actually *encourage* overeating. Dieting makes people vulnerable to binges by creating physical and psychological pressures to eat. Parts Two and Three of this course will show you how this happens and how to break the vicious circle.

Vomiting

The great majority of people with bulimia nervosa compensate for overeating by making themselves vomit. Like binge-eating, this is done privately and in secret.

'I started vomiting after eating too much chocolate one day. It seemed a brilliant way of staying thin without dieting. I could eat as much as I wanted and then get rid of it. It would be so much easier than all that dieting.'

Typically, vomiting is induced by sticking the fingers or another object down the throat to set off the gag reflex. About a quarter of people with bulimia nervosa who vomit have voluntary control over the gag reflex: that is, they are able to vomit at will simply by leaning forward or by pressing their hand on their stomach.

'I first started vomiting as a way of eating what I liked, without feeling guilty and without putting on weight. Vomiting was surprisingly easy and I was pretty pleased with myself. It was only later that I realized what a problem it had become.'

How often people with bulimia nervosa induce vomiting varies considerably:

- Some people make themselves vomit repeatedly, many times in one day, both after binges and after having eaten anything they regard as fattening. It is not uncommon for people to be vomiting ten times a day.

- After a binge, some people vomit just once, while others will do so again and again, sometimes for up to an hour. This process is physically and emotionally exhausting.

- Some use a 'flushing' technique: they vomit, drink water, vomit again, drink again, and so on; and they repeat this process until the water returns clear and they feel sure that they have eliminated all the food they possibly can. This can be physically harmful.

'I eat until I literally cannot eat any more. Then, using my fingers, I make myself sick. Over the next half-hour, drinking water between vomits, I purge all the food from my stomach. I then feel despondent, depressed, alone and desperately scared because I have lost control again. I feel physically terrible: exhausted, puffy-eyed, dizzy, weak, and my throat hurts. I am also scared because I know it is dangerous.'

As with dieting, although vomiting starts out as a way of trying to control weight, it ends up having the opposite effect. This may happen in one of two ways.

- Usually, people begin to make themselves vomit as a response to having lost control of their eating.

- Many people say that when they first discovered that they could vomit after eating, they felt quite elated, thinking they could now eat what they liked without gaining weight.

- However, this elation doesn't last long, because it soon becomes clear that, by removing the psychological and physical barriers restricting eating, vomiting actually encourages overeating.

- Also, the process of vomiting is easier following the consumption of large rather than small amounts of food; so the size of binges increases.

- Vomiting therefore leads to more frequent binge-eating, and to eating more and more in each binge.

Or:

- Some people who binge originally got into the habit of vomiting before starting to experience loss of control over eating, using vomiting on top of dieting as a method of weight control.

- People who do this often find that at first it seems to work; that is, that they lose some weight.

- However, soon the combination of weight loss and hunger drives them to overeat.

- They respond by further vomiting, which in turn leads to more overeating.

'Over the past eight years I have repeatedly said to myself "This is going to be the last time that I throw up". At first I was not that bothered: I thought I could control it, if I chose to. But it soon became clear that it had control over me. Now stopping seems completely beyond my reach.'

Some people who find it difficult to vomit induce nausea 'chemically' by drinking salt water, or occasionally domestic chemicals, such as shampoo. Others take syrup of ipecac. All these practices are dangerous and have toxic effects.

There are a number of reasons why vomiting should not be used as a means of weight control.

- It can be physically damaging, even dangerous.

- It can be just as damaging psychologically, bringing on feelings of shame and guilt.

- It often becomes a habit which is difficult to break.

- It doesn't work. Most calories consumed in a binge may be eliminated by vomiting, but a significant proportion are absorbed. Given that binges frequently consist of large amounts of food, the proportion absorbed can amount to a lot of calories. In fact, many people who binge and vomit frequently, and attempt to fast between binges, maintain their body weight largely by the calories they absorb from binges.

Misusing laxatives and diuretics

About one in five people with bulimia nervosa attempt to compensate for having binged by taking laxatives, in the belief that this will prevent food being absorbed into the body.

> *'I started taking laxatives because I was scared that because I was eating so much I would get fat really quickly. I thought that if I took laxatives all the food would go straight through me.'*

As with vomiting, this is a bad idea, for several reasons:

- If laxatives are taken regularly, the body gets used to them, and higher and higher doses are needed to produce an effect. Some people end up taking considerable quantities (up to 100 times the normal dose). This can damage the digestive system.

- The body responds to the taking of laxatives by trying harder to retain fluid. This leads to oedema (water retention), which causes puffiness round the eyes and general swelling, especially around the wrists and ankles.

- It doesn't work. Laxatives act on the lower portion of the gut, and calories contained in the food eaten are absorbed higher up in the digestive system.

> *'The hardest thing after a binge is waiting for the effects to die down. I hate feeling so useless and unable to do anything. Sometimes I feel I could literally rip open my stomach and pull out the garbage inside, the disgust and revulsion is so great. Failing that, laxatives are the next best thing.'*

Some people use diuretics ('water tablets') instead of, or as well as, laxatives, as a means of reducing their weight. However, diuretics have no impact at all on body weight. The small effect they seem to have is solely due to fluid loss; and this 'weight loss' is rapidly reversed when, in response to dehydration, fluids are consumed. Likewise, there is no evidence to suggest that appetite suppressant drugs ('diet pills') work to reduce binge-eating.

Attitudes to weight and shape

For many people who binge, and all of those with bulimia nervosa, how they feel about their weight and shape determines more than anything else how they feel about themselves. Little else, if anything, has so great an effect on their sense of self-worth.

> *'I am confident in many ways, yet I hate my body and can't bear to look at it. I feel bloated, wobbly and huge all over. This drives me to binge. My boyfriend loves me. Why can't I like myself?'*

- Concerns about their shape and weight dominate their lives.

- Many are consumed by a powerful desire to lose weight and become thin.

> *'My confidence and feelings of self-worth are deeply rooted in the idea that I must be physically attractive, i.e. thin. When I put on weight, even one pound, I risk being unattractive, and I see my future as bleak and lonely. This thought fills me with despair, so I force myself to eat as little as possible.'*

- If they think they have gained weight or have become fat, they see this as a catastrophe and it has a profound effect on their lives. They feel deeply depressed, avoid company and give up attempting to control their eating.

- As a consequence they binge, become more depressed and fiercely attempt to renew their efforts to diet and lose weight.

- If, on the other hand, they find they have lost weight they can feel quite elated.

- Most are acutely sensitive to small changes in weight and shape which are, in truth, undetectable by ordinary means.

> *'I am obsessed with my weight. I weigh myself over and over again, sometimes up to fifteen times a day. At other times I am so disgusted with my body that I don't use the scales for weeks or months at a time.'*

Read through the following list of statements people with bulimia nervosa have made about their weight and shape, and how they feel about them, and tick all those you find yourself agreeing with:

☐ 'If I feel bad about my weight and shape I feel bad about myself generally.'

☐ 'If I have put on even a small amount of weight, I feel really depressed.'

☐ 'If I feel fat, I don't like to go out among people.'

☐ 'I feel happiest about my shape in the morning, when I haven't eaten anything.'

☐   'If I see my reflection in a shop window I always feel bad about my shape.'

☐   'If I feel full after a meal I think I'm fat.'

It is these concerns, and the belief that self-worth depends on weight and shape, that drive the disturbed eating habits of people with bulimia nervosa. If you believe that self-worth depends on being thin, dieting follows quite logically. And, again, it is understandable why people who hold this belief feel the need to take extreme measures (such as vomiting) if overeating has occurred.

Most people with bulimia nervosa don't like their bodies and at the same time have a distorted view of them.

- Even if their weight is perfectly 'normal', they feel certain parts of their body (for example, the stomach, bottom and hips) to be too fat. This often causes great distress and spurs them on to more intense dieting.

- At the same time, they tend to overestimate their actual size: that is to say, they see their body as larger than it actually is.

- On top of this, they have an unrealistically small 'ideal' size.

  'I cannot put into words how repulsed I am with my body. I wish it were possible to wear clothes that disguised one's shape completely. I cannot bear to look at my body and will have no mirrors in the house. I take showers instead of baths to avoid having to look at myself. I have not gone shopping for clothes for more than three years.'

SECTION 2: How Do Binge-Eating and Bulimia Nervosa Affect People?

Bulimia nervosa and binge-eating have serious effects on people's

- state of mind: many have symptoms of depression and anxiety, and feel angry with themselves;
- social life: for many, this becomes very restricted;
- physical health: this may be damaged by bingeing and by attempts to compensate for binges.

'My life revolves around my eating. I can no longer concentrate on my work, which has suffered greatly as a result. My problem has caused family rows. I no longer enjoy sharing meals with family or friends. I have become withdrawn and introspective and have lost all self-confidence and self-respect. I don't want to go out. I don't like myself any more.'

The effects on state of mind

Symptoms of depression

We saw in the previous section that the self-esteem of people who binge is intimately bound up with how they see their body shape and weight. So, if they believe their weight or shape is unacceptable, they feel they are worthless. This makes it particularly humiliating for them periodically to lose control of their eating and overeat. They feel intensely ashamed and disgusted at themselves for being unable to maintain control over their eating. At times they feel utterly desolate and quite hopeless about ever being able to improve how they eat.

It's not surprising, then, that many people who binge experience symptoms of depression. Table 1 overleaf shows how often such symptoms occurred in one group of people with bulimia nervosa who came for treatment. The figures in the table are based on patients' responses to a standardized psychiatric interview designed to detect the presence of symptoms severe enough to have a marked negative effect on functioning.

Table 1: Symptoms of depression in a group of patients with bulimia nervosa

Symptom	Frequency (%)
Feelings of guilt	94
Poor concentration	80
Feelings of worthlessness	74
Irritability	71
Lack of energy	71
Loss of self-confidence	66
Depressed mood	63
Social withdrawal	63
Feelings of hopelessness	60

It is clear from this table that a wide range of depressive symptoms are common in those with bulimia nervosa. These symptoms are directly linked to the core disturbances in eating and the patients' concerns about their shape and weight, as the following list shows:

Guilt	because of:	shame about binge-eating and vomiting
Worthlessness	because of:	feelings of failure to control eating and achieve a desired weight and shape
Social withdrawal	because of:	feeling weight and shape unacceptable

Many people who binge at times feel quite desperate. They hate what they are doing, they despise themselves, and they can see little, if any, prospect of their situation improving. In these circumstances, some attempt suicide, usually by taking an overdose of pills. Around one in twenty of those with bulimia nervosa coming for treatment in Britain has at some time taken an overdose.

The great majority of people who binge find that their depressive symptoms disappear once they have regained control over their eating habits. However, a few suffer a depressive disorder that is independent of the disturbance in eating. For these people, depressive symptoms remain severe and disabling even if their eating disorder improves. It is important that these people, as well as getting help in overcoming their problems with eating, receive specific treatment for their depression. A good first step would be to read Paul Gilbert's book *Overcoming Depression* – for full details see the 'Useful Information' section at the end of Part Three.

Symptoms of anxiety

Many people who binge have distressing symptoms of anxiety. These include the mental symptoms of worrying and anxious foreboding, as well as physical symptoms such as palpitations, sweating, difficulty in breathing and churning of the stomach. Table 2 shows how often some of these symptoms occurred in a group of patients with bulimia nervosa. As in table 1, the percentages show how many patients experienced these symptoms severely enough to have a marked effect on their lives.

Table 2: Symptoms of anxiety in a group of patients with bulimia nervosa	
Symptom	**Frequency (%)**
Worrying	69
Tension pains (e.g. tension headaches)	68
Nervous tension (i.e. keyed up, on edge)	68
Active avoidance of anxiety-provoking situations	62
Anxiety when meeting people	51
Anxiety in specific situations	48
Panic attacks	10

As with depressive symptoms in people who binge, these anxiety symptoms are closely linked to the core disorder of eating:

Worrying	because of:	concerns about food, eating, shape and weight
Anxiety in specific situations	because of:	concerns about there being food around or feelings of being fat

These anxiety symptoms only rarely require separate treatment from the eating problems. That is, if the eating disorder is brought under control, the anxiety tends to lift spontaneously. Nevertheless, if anxiety is a problem for you, you may find it helpful to read *Overcoming Anxiety* by Helen Kennerley (for details see the 'Useful Information' section at the end of Part Three).

Feelings of anger

Many people who binge feel extremely angry with themselves and want to punish themselves. This self-punishment can take various forms:

- Some people take laxatives after a binge not only to try to get rid of the food but because they have unpleasant physical effects.

- Others punish themselves even more drastically, for example hitting themselves with a belt, a rope or even a hammer.

- Others cut themselves. Usually the cutting or scratching causes only minor skin wounds, with some bleeding. In some cases, however, the cutting is much more serious, with deep wounds being made into muscles.

The effects on social life

Binge-eating is a particularly lonely activity:

- Binge-eating is done in private and kept secret.

- Attempts to compensate by vomiting and taking laxatives cause guilt and shame.

- This in turn tends to make people determined to keep their disturbed eating habits completely secret.

- This has the effect of isolating them, because a central part of their existence is kept hidden away from those with whom they live and otherwise share their lives.

   'My eating problem has taken over my whole life. My friendships have been upset by my violent swings in mood. I never talk to my parents since they have never under-stood what I am going through, yet we were so close. I have so little self-confidence. I get terribly depressed and anxious. I can't face seeing people.'

Mixing with other people

Concerns about shape and weight also have a direct effect on social life. Many people with bulimia nervosa will mix socially when they feel reasonably happy about their weight and shape; but the moment they binge or feel they have gained weight or become fat, they withdraw completely. Some will literally hide away for days at a time, refusing to see anyone, or to allow anyone to see them.

Eating with other people

Much of ordinary social life takes place around food and eating:

- Friends meet in bars or restaurants and at each others' homes for meals.

- Families eat together both routinely and for special occasions.

Even these everyday situations worry, sometimes even terrify, people who binge. So they try to avoid them – and in doing so cut themselves off from 'normal' social life.

Family life

Bulimia nervosa and binge-eating can seriously disrupt family life:

- Someone who binges or has bulimia nervosa often goes through rapid mood swings and gets very irritable at times. Spouses, parents, partners and children find themselves on the receiving end of these emotional effects.

- Family social arrangements are often upset, maybe at short notice and seemingly for no reason.

- Family meals can be particularly difficult.

- Feeding children, especially very young children, can be very difficult for someone with binge-eating problems. If you are having such difficulties, you should discuss these with your family doctor.

Money

Binge-eating can be very expensive, and many people who binge, especially those who are doing it often, find themselves facing a problem in paying for the food they eat. Some find themselves taking food belonging to others; some steal food and other items from shops. As well as adding to the shame they feel and the drive to keep the habit secret, this can cause arguments with friends and relatives; and, of course, if stealing is involved it sometimes leads to prosecution in the courts.

Have a look at the following list of statements made by people with bulimia nervosa. Tick any that you recognize as similar to things you have thought.

☐ 'I am very reserved with my friends because I'm afraid if I open up I might blurt out something about my eating.'

☐ 'I don't make arrangements to see friends in case when the time comes I've had a binge and feel dreadful.'

☐ 'I know my family find me difficult to live with and that makes me feel even worse.'

☐ 'I hate group meals out because I'm scared they'll make me binge afterwards.'

☐ 'I can't tell my partner that I'm struggling with money because of what I spend on food, and that makes me feel so low and deceitful.'

The social rewards of recovery

The social and personal lives of people who binge are transformed when they recover from the disorder. So much of ordinary life that had previously been closed to them is opened up:

- They are able to socialize freely.

- Intimate personal relationships become much easier and more fulfilling.

- Family life becomes much happier.

The physical effects

Physical effects of binge-eating

Binges usually produce a sense of fullness and bloatedness. This can cause:

- pain in the stomach, which is sometimes severe;

- breathlessness, because the distended stomach is pressing against the diaphragm.

In rare cases, the stomach wall can be damaged and even tear. This is a serious medical emergency.

General digestive problems are common among people who binge. These include:

- stomach cramps;

- flatulence;

- constipation;

- diarrhoea.

The physical effects of trying to compensate for binges

Self-induced vomiting

Making yourself vomit has a number of adverse physical effects, some of which can be medically serious.

- Teeth start to lose their enamel, mainly on the inner surface, because they are repeatedly being exposed to acid from the stomach. Many people brush their teeth vigorously after vomiting, to get rid of the smell; this actually makes things worse, scouring the teeth with the acid in the mouth. The damage caused to the teeth by repeated vomiting cannot be undone.

- Vomiting causes the salivary glands below the jaw to swell. This is painless, but it makes the face look rather puffy; this is particularly distressing to someone with bulimia nervosa, who is apt to interpret the swelling as a sign of weight gain and may well respond with further vomiting.

- Repeated vomiting often causes damage to the throat. This is because most people make themselves vomit by sticking something down their throat. Setting off the gag reflex in this way can be difficult and some people have to use considerable force. The back of the throat is often injured in this process. Sometimes it bleeds and the injuries often become infected. People who vomit frequently may develop a hoarseness in their voice.

- Very rarely, violent vomiting causes a tear in the oesophagus (the tube linking the mouth to the stomach). This is a medical emergency.

- Vomiting repeatedly for many years can also weaken the oesophageal sphincter (the set of muscles at the top of the stomach), so that there is nothing to prevent the contents of the stomach from returning up the oesophagus into the mouth (so-called gastric reflux). This can be uncomfortable, distressing and embarrassing.

- When people 'flush' their stomachs by repeatedly vomiting, drinking, and vomiting again until they are satisfied that their stomach is empty of food, they upset the balance of body fluids and body salts (electrolytes). Often this doesn't cause any symptoms, but the effects can be serious, especially if the level of potassium falls too low (this is called hypokalemia), because it can result in serious heartbeat irregularities. Electrolyte disturbance is reversible, however, and the effects disappear once vomiting stops.

Misusing laxatives and diuretics

Misuse of laxatives and diuretics can causes several problems:

- People may become dependent on them and need to take larger and larger doses to achieve the desired effect.

- Stopping taking them can be difficult, because the body becomes used to them and the shock of withdrawal leads to 'rebound' constipation (with laxatives) and water retention (with laxatives and diuretics). Like vomiting, laxative and diuretic misuse can cause fluid and electrolyte abnormalities – so this can be a particular risk to people who both vomit and take laxatives/diuretics.

- Some laxatives, when taken in large doses, can cause damage to the gut wall.

Apart from the last of these problems, the physical consequences of laxative and diuretic misuse disappear rapidly once you stop taking them.

Appetite suppressants

Appetite suppressants can cause agitation or depression. They are not to be recommended for people who binge.

The physical rewards of recovery

Most people who come for treatment of bulimia nervosa or binge-eating have been overeating and vomiting for some years. By this time many will have suffered some damage to their teeth. However, they are most unlikely to have caused themselves any other permanent physical harm. When they restore their eating habits to normal their bodies soon return to a healthy state.

SECTION 3: What Causes Binge-Eating and Bulimia Nervosa?

'I had been anorexic for about a year and was attempting to start eating properly. One day, out of the blue, I ate a chocolate biscuit. Suddenly I began eating all these things I'd deprived myself of. It wasn't a large binge by my current standards, but it was more calories than I normally ate in a whole week. I came out of my trance-like state and was suddenly terrified about what I had done. I immediately went to the bathroom and stuck my fingers down my throat. I had to throw up and get rid of all the garbage inside me.'

The causes of medical conditions are rarely simple, and the causes of psychological problems such as depression, anxiety and eating disorders are even more complicated, and that much more difficult to understand.

It is helpful, when trying to understand the causes of a disorder, to divide up the various factors into three groups:

* things that make people vulnerable to the disorder;

* things that bring on the disorder; and

* things that, once the disorder has become established, maintain it or prevent sufferers from recovering spontaneously.

In the rest of this section these three sorts of factors will be discussed to put together a picture of what may make a person prone to develop bulimia nervosa and binge-eating, what can actually bring on the problems, and what can make them continue.

What makes a person vulnerable to binge-eating and bulimia nervosa?

Physical factors

A tendency towards eating disorders may be in part inherited. Two types of evidence support this view:

* Eating disorders run in families.

- Where one of a pair of twins has an eating disorder, if the twins are identical (that is, share the same genes) rather than non-identical, it is much more likely that the other twin will also have an eating disorder.

However, both of these facts could also be explained in terms of the family environment rather than in terms of physical heredity. Family members, after all, largely share the same environment; and it could be this common experience that explains why eating disorders run in families. Again, identical twins are likely to share the same environment to a greater extent than non-identical twins, and it may be this, rather than shared genes, that accounts for the high occurrence of eating disorders in both of a pair of identical twins.

Some think that an inherited tendency to depression might raise the risk of developing an eating disorder. This suggestion is based on two facts:

- Depression is common among the family members of people with eating disorders.

- About a third of people with an eating disorder have themselves experienced an episode of depression before the onset of their eating disorder.

However, it is not at all clear how this link might work. Also, if there is a link it might be psychological rather than physical. That is, the child of a depressed parent might be more likely to have low self-esteem, which might then make the child vulnerable to the development of an eating disorder.

Finally, inheritance might contribute to causing binge-eating and bulimia nervosa in terms of the genetic transmission of body weight.

- There is good evidence that inheritance has a significant influence on how much one weighs as an adult.

- Many people who binge have a tendency to have a higher than average natural weight. Indeed, nearly half of those with bulimia nervosa have been significantly overweight before the onset of their eating problems.

- This suggests that a tendency to be overweight makes a person vulnerable to the development of bulimia nervosa and binge-eating. Such a tendency might contribute to the onset of eating problems when combined with some of the psychological and social factors that we shall now look at.

Psychological factors

About a third of people who develop bulimia nervosa do so following an episode of anorexia nervosa. This tends to happen in one of two ways:

- Some people with anorexia nervosa lose control of their eating after a period where they have successfully kept their calorie intake low; as a consequence, their weight rises and they become desperate to get it down again.

- Others have always had binge-eating episodes as part of their anorexia nervosa, but at some point the frequency and size of binges increase and they gain weight – with the same result.

We don't know precisely how anorexia nervosa raises the risk of bulimia nervosa. It might be largely physical; for example, it may be starvation itself which leads to binge-eating. Or the chain of cause and effect might be psychological: for example, dieting and preoccupations with food may raise the risk of episodes of loss of control. Or a combination of physical and psychological factors might be involved.

Certain psychological characteristics appear to make people vulnerable to developing an eating disorder. Two of the main ones are:

- low self-esteem; and

- a tendency towards perfectionism.

In some cases, low self-esteem and a profound sense of ineffectiveness appear to have roots in past experience, such as an unhappy family. About a third of people with bulimia nervosa report having been sexually abused. This fact has led some to conclude that childhood sexual abuse is a specific cause of eating disorders. However, this is not the case, because childhood sexual abuse is just as commonly reported by people with other psychiatric disorders such as depression but without eating problems. Such abuse is clearly psychologically damaging, but it does not appear to lead to a specific type of disorder.

People who develop eating disorders often set very high standards for themselves and strive extremely hard to meet their goals.

The combination of these two elements of perfectionism and a sense of ineffectiveness seems to make people vulnerable to developing an eating disorder.

It is also worth noting that a history of problems with alcohol has also been found to make people vulnerable to the development of an eating disorder.

Social factors

Three observations suggest that social factors are important in making some people vulnerable to developing eating disorders:

● Binge-eating and bulimia nervosa only occur in certain cultures.

● The overwhelming majority of people who suffer from these problems are women.

● Eating disorders are especially common in certain social groups, such as ballet dancers and fashion models, where there is a strong emphasis on an ideal of thinness.

Fashion models have become progressively thinner in recent decades, and at the same time eating disorders have become more widespread. There is no way of telling for certain whether this association is a purely accidental one. But it certainly might not be. We know that a habit of dieting increases the risk of developing an eating disorder; so, if the presentation of thin fashion models in the media increases the number of girls and women who go on diets, then it is also likely that it is responsible for more girls and women developing eating disorders.

In fact, the current fashion industry projects an image of women which is positively unhealthy. An article in the *British Medical Journal* observed from a study of the fashion mannequins we see in shop windows that these models are so thin that, if they were flesh and blood, they would fail to menstruate! A number of feminist writers have argued persuasively that the pressures women are under to be thin are a tyranny which they should fiercely resist.

There are also social factors at work within the family that might make some girls vulnerable to developing eating disorders. For example, concerns about shape and weight may be passed on from mothers to their daughters. Certainly, the daughters of women who diet are likely to diet themselves. In addition, people with eating disorders describe their family relationships as much more disturbed than do people with no psychiatric problems. However, it is uncertain whether these relationship difficulties precede the onset of the eating problems or arise as a consequence of them.

What brings on binge-eating and bulimia nervosa?

Physical factors

Some cases of binge-eating and bulimia nervosa begin after a person loses weight following an episode of physical illness. She might find that her friends remark admiringly on her thinner appearance, and that this gives her a sense of achievement and social acceptability. This in turn may give her a powerful desire to diet in the attempt to keep her new weight and shape and thereby preserve this sense of approval.

Psychological factors

The single most important factor in bringing on binge-eating and bulimia nervosa is a period of dieting.

The great majority of those who binge can recall clearly a period of dieting, which may or may not have led to weight loss, before the first occasion on which they lost control over their eating.

There's a paradox here. You might well expect that people with extreme concerns about their shape and weight who break their dietary rules in small ways would respond by dieting more strictly. However, people who binge react in the opposite way – by abandoning their efforts at dieting altogether, and overeating instead.

Given this paradoxical response of people who diet and binge, it may be that it is the dieting itself which actually causes the episodes of loss of control. This argument certainly fits with the accounts that people with bulimia nervosa themselves give. It also fits with laboratory studies of how people who diet eat. For example, if people who are not dieting drink a high-calorie milk shake (a so-called 'preload') and then are asked to rate the taste and texture of certain foods, they will eat smaller amounts of those foods in order to make their ratings than they would if they had not had the milk shake. People who are dieting, on the other hand, behave in exactly the opposite way: they will eat more in the tasting session if they have had a high-calorie 'preload' before the session than if they have not had one. What is more, this happens if they believe they have had a high-calorie drink, even if, in fact, the drink contained few calories. This strongly suggests that the effect is largely driven by psychological factors.

Other factors that prompt dieters to eat more are:

- depressed mood, and

- the consumption of alcohol.

What these provocation factors appear to have in common is that they undermine a dieter's resolve to resist eating.

However, although dieting does appear to be important in setting off binge-eating, it is not at all clear why, among the great number of people who diet, some lose control of their eating and others do not.

Some people who binge insist that they were not dieting before they began to lose control over eating. In these people, binge-eating appears to have served a particular psychological function. They may have overeaten in response to stress; or they may have used eating as a way of blotting out unacceptable feelings of misery or anger.

Social factors

Some people who binge can clearly remember a social situation or experience that originally provoked a disturbance in their eating habits. For example, a woman might decide to start dieting

- after being rejected by a potential boyfriend;

- after being teased about being fat;

- to conform when her friends go on diets.

Many people can remember social circumstances like these as reasons why they started dieting, and they clearly identify these points as the beginning of their problems with eating. However, few can think of social factors that were directly relevant to the onset of their binge-eating.

What keeps the vicious circle going?

Physical factors

Being significantly below one's natural or healthy body weight itself keeps eating disorders going, in a number of interlinking ways:

- a low weight leads to preoccupation with food and eating, and

- causes depressive symptoms;

- these symptoms lower self-esteem further, leading to

- social withdrawal,

- a reduction in outside interests, and, sometimes,

- a loss of interest in sex.

All these changes increase isolation and remove the stabilizing influence of ordinary social life.

A low weight also

- places the body under physiological pressures to eat, regardless of the cause of the weight loss, and

- disrupts the normal physiological processes that control eating.

Psychological factors

The diagram overleaf shows how a number of psychological factors interlink with one another to keep binge-eating and bulimia nervosa going. First, look at the downward arrows on the right-hand side of the figure.

- At the root of bulimia nervosa, as we have already seen, is a profound lack of self-esteem.

- This leads vulnerable people, such as women with a tendency to be overweight in a society where slimness is linked to success, to have extreme concerns about shape and weight.

- Driven by these concerns, they go on strict diets.

- The dieting then encourages overeating, through both physiological and psychological mechanisms, leading to episodes of binge-eating.

- The binge-eating in turn leads to extreme action to compensate for the overeating, such as self-induced vomiting (and laxative and diuretic misuse).

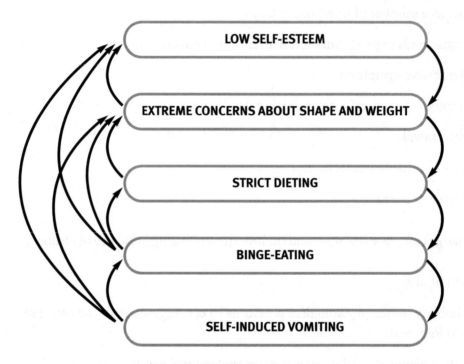

Source: Adapted from C. G. Fairburn and P. J. Cooper, 'Eating Disorders', in K. Hawton, P. Salkovskis, J. Kirk and D. M. Clark, eds, *Cognitive Behaviour Therapy for Psychiatric Problems: A Practical Guide*, Oxford, Oxford University Press, 1989.

Now look at the upward-pointing arrows on the left-hand side of the diagram.

- Vomiting (and, to a lesser extent, laxative and diuretic misuse) encourages further overeating, because it seems to remove the need to resist urges to eat.

- Vomiting heightens preoccupations with shape and weight, as do binge-eating and dieting.

- Finally, self-induced vomiting (and laxative and diuretic misuse), binge-eating, and extreme concerns about shape and weight, all serve to undermine people's sense of self-control and self-esteem.

- This adds to feelings of ineffectiveness and intensifies concerns about shape and weight, and the cycle thereby repeats itself.

Social factors

The beliefs of people with bulimia nervosa about the importance of shape and weight are reinforced by the norms of Western society. There is a huge amount of advertising in women's magazines and on television glorifying female thinness and encouraging the idea that, for a woman, to be thin is a marker of success. It is difficult, against this tide of propaganda, to convince women that body shape and weight are not really important. In this sense, our culture encourages preoccupations with shape and weight in women, and it rewards successful dieting.

SECTION 4: Is the Self-Help Programme For You?

Identifying the problem

If you have read this far because you have problems with your eating, it should now be clear to you whether or not you have bulimia nervosa or some variation of this disorder. Similarly, if you have a friend or relative with bulimia nervosa, you should by now have an idea of the sorts of problems they experience with eating, and the kinds of effects these problems will be having on their life.

If you have problems controlling your eating, the question will now arise: What should you do about it?

Working out what to do next

Many people who have problems controlling their eating manage to overcome their difficulties without seeking professional help. For some it is fairly straightforward, for others it is very difficult; but somehow they do succeed. They manage to stop binge-eating. They stop making themselves sick. They stop taking laxatives. They eat ordinary meals at regular times. And, most important of all, food and eating cease to dominate their lives and they stop being so intensely concerned about their weight and their shape. In other words, they start to lead 'normal' lives again.

Sadly, many other people with very similar problems find themselves referred to specialist clinics having been unable, after repeated efforts, to manage on their own. It is not necessarily that their problems have been around longer or that their eating habits are more severely disturbed. It is just that the things they tried to do to improve matters simply did not work. And often they made things considerably worse.

Now, of course, many people with bulimia nervosa will need specialist help and it is important that they seek such help and get it. But many others could, if they knew how to go about it, manage to restore their eating habits to normal on their own. This self-help course is intended to provide guidelines for people who want to try to manage on their own but are unsure where to begin.

Is this course suitable for you?

The guidelines set out in Parts Two and Three of this course are aimed at people who have what might be termed 'classic bulimia nervosa' – that is to say, people who:

- regularly lose control of their eating and binge;

- attempt to compensate for the episodes of overeating in extreme ways (e.g. by fasting, vomiting or taking laxatives); and

- regard their body shape or weight as of great personal significance, to the extent that concerns about weight and shape dominate their lives.

Of course, there are many other people who do not quite fit this description but who share some of the same features:

- they may binge occasionally;

- they may not binge, but regularly make themselves sick after meals or after eating any food they believe to be fattening;

- they may alternate between periods of relatively normal eating and days of strict fasting to lose weight;

- they may regularly take laxatives to compensate for eating what they regard as fattening food.

The course that follows is also likely to be useful to these people. Although some parts of it may not be relevant to them, the general principles apply to all people who are experiencing difficulty controlling their eating, and who want to restore their disturbed eating habits to normal and to put their concerns about their weight and shape into a manageable perspective.

What if this course is not suitable for you?

There are six kinds of people with bulimia nervosa for whom this course is probably not the best route to recovery.

- Some people are rigidly locked into a pattern of grossly disturbed eating habits. For them, the idea of being able to break out of the cycle on their own may not be realistic. It is important to add here that many people who do not belong to this category will think that they do. If you are prepared just to *try* to change some aspects of your current eating habits, then you probably do not belong to this category.

- Some people who are completely socially isolated may well need the support and encouragement of a therapist they can see regularly.

- Some people who are so demoralized and disheartened that they cannot muster up the energy to begin to try to change will probably need more personal help than this programme can provide.

- For some the eating disorder is only one relatively minor feature of much wider difficulties, such as problems with alcohol, self-harm (such as cutting themselves or repeatedly taking overdoses) and their relationships; they too will need more help than is provided in this course.

- For some people whose body weight is very low (and, in addition to bulimia nervosa, are suffering from anorexia nervosa), it is possible that the guidelines contained in this manual could actually be harmful rather than improving matters.

- People with a medical condition in which eating can have a significant impact (such as diabetes), and women who are pregnant, need medical care.

If you belong to one or more of these six categories you will need specialist help and you should consult your doctor about being referred for treatment. For all of these groups specific treatments are available, and the prospects of being helped are good if such treatment is received.

How likely is the course to help you?

This course is likely to help the great majority of those with bulimia nervosa and related problems. This statement can be made with confidence because the effectiveness of the manual on which it is based has been studied. When this manual was originally developed, it was given to more than eighty people with bulimia nervosa who had been referred for treatment by their doctors. They used it for four to six months and were then re-evaluated. The great majority of them had improved substantially and regarded themselves as no longer in need of help. More recently, a carefully controlled study of the manual carried out in Australia has confirmed these early promising results.*

* The reference for the paper reporting this study is: Susan J. Banasiah, Susan J. Paxton and Philippa Hay, 'Guided self-help for bulimia nervosa in primary care: a randomised controlled trial', *Psychological Medicine* 35 (2005), 1283–94.

Some points to consider before you start

Making change a high priority

Overcoming difficulties with eating is seldom easy and is usually very hard indeed. So if you are going to make a serious effort at doing so, you will have to make this task more important than anything else you are doing.

Restoring your eating habits to normal must be your first priority, and other responsibilities will have to fall in line behind it.

This may sound like awful advice. You may well feel that it is totally against your principles to act so 'selfishly'. But in fact it is the most responsible thing to do, because it is only by overcoming your eating problems that you can properly take on your wider personal and social commitments. So, if you feel reluctant to give your own problems such a high priority at the expense of the needs of others, you can reassure yourself that it would really be in everyone else's best interests if you did so.

Why is it worth changing?

While it is true that it is difficult to overcome bulimia nervosa, doing so is immensely worthwhile. To most people this is so obvious that it is hardly worth saying. But some people might need a certain amount of convincing. So let's revisit the effects of bulimia nervosa discussed in Section 2, focusing this time on the benefits to be gained from leaving them behind.

Psychological reasons

First, a summary of the psychological consequences of bulimia nervosa:

- Binge-eating and vomiting lead to feelings of shame and guilt.

- These feelings lead people to live a secret and lonely existence, sometimes for many years, and make them believe they are inferior to others – even, at times, quite worthless.

- Severe depression commonly sets in after a binge, and this can last for some time.

- Some people undergo wild mood swings, usually in response to their degree of control over their eating, switching rapidly from feeling extremely happy to feeling utterly miserable.

- Often people feel very anxious in situations involving exposure to food, such as eating out, eating in front of others, or preparing food for other people.

- The constant preoccupation with weight, shape, food and eating often makes concentrating difficult.

- It is common for people to feel that their lives are totally dominated by thoughts about food and eating and concerns about weight and shape.

Reinstating 'normal' eating habits reverses many of these difficulties and is a major step towards resolving the others. Look at the following list of psychological benefits of recovering from bulimia nervosa and tick all those you would like to apply to you:

☐ No longer feeling guilty and ashamed about eating habits.

☐ No longer having to be secretive about eating habits.

☐ Having higher self-esteem.

☐ Being less depressed.

☐ No longer having severe mood swings.

☐ Being able to eat out, eat with others, and entertain guests to meals without feeling anxious.

☐ Being able to concentrate on other areas of life without being constantly preoccupied with weight, shape, food and eating.

Social reasons

Bulimia nervosa takes a great toll in terms of one's social life:

- Personal relationships are badly affected.

- At worst, binge-eating and vomiting occur many times a day and there is simply no time to lead anything like a normal life.

- Much of social life involves eating with other people, and many people with bulimia nervosa feel unable to do this, so end up always eating on their own.

- People often feel fat and unattractive after a binge and don't want to be seen by anyone. So they avoid company and again choose to remain on their own. Unfortunately, under these circumstances they are much more likely to binge.

- Family relationships frequently become strained.

- At work, it can be very difficult to deal with the cafeteria or coffee breaks.

- Thoughts of food and eating and concerns about weight and shape can damage concentration so that work performance suffers.

- Even if one is apparently coping quite well, the feelings of depression and worth-lessness which the binge-eating and vomiting cause can make one feel generally inadequate and unconfident at work and socially.

Again, all these difficulties improve considerably when one's eating habits return to normal. Look at the following list of social benefits of recovering from bulimia nervosa and tick all those you would like to apply to you:

☐ Marked improvement in personal relationships.

☐ Time to lead a normal life with normal social activities.

☐ Feeling able to eat with other people.

☐ More relaxed family relationships.

☐ Less anxiety about food breaks at work.

☐ Less anxiety about performance at work.

☐ More social confidence, at work and among friends, family and strangers.

Medical reasons

There are a number of medical complications that can arise as a result of bulimia nervosa and binge-eating. Some of these result from the binge-eating itself, others from the methods used to compensate for overeating (vomiting, taking laxatives, and so on).

Some of these complications are common, such as

- abdominal pain;

- damage to tooth enamel;

- swollen salivary glands;

- sore throats.

Others, though rare, are more serious, such as

- damage to the stomach wall;
- damage to the oesophagus;
- hypokalemia (low potassium) as a result of repeated vomiting and laxative-taking, leading to irregularities in heartbeat.

Look at the following list of physical benefits of recovering from bulimia nervosa and tick all those you would like to apply to you:

☐ Far less frequent abdominal pain and sore throats.

☐ Healthier mouth and throat.

☐ An end to fear of damaging internal organs.

☐ No need to worry about possible irregularities in heartbeat.

Other personal reasons

The previous paragraphs have set out some of the reasons why it is worthwhile committing yourself to overcoming your eating difficulties. No doubt there are other reasons why you as an individual want to do this, and perhaps they are even more compelling. Write them down here:

_____

_____

_____

_____

_____

_____

_____

_____

_____

Whatever your particular reasons for wishing to change, it is important to empha-size right at the beginning that *you will not be able to stop binge-eating and resume 'normal' eating unless you are very highly motivated to do so*. By the same token, if you really want to change and are prepared to make this your top priority for a period, there is every reason to expect that you will be successful.

'Why can't I just stop binge-eating?'

Before you set out on the self-help programme, it is worth looking at what prevents people with bulimia nervosa from just getting better spontaneously. After all, it may seem odd that people with bulimia nervosa behave as they do when it is so contrary to how they want to behave and when it makes them so miserable.

The reason why this happens is that people unwittingly adopt methods of coping that are counter-productive. For example, fasting after a binge may make you feel better temporarily, but it also significantly increases the chances that you will binge again.

We have already touched on what keeps bulimia nervosa going (see pages 27–9), but it is worth looking in a bit more detail here at the main factors.

The truth about dieting

Most young women at some time go on a diet to lose weight. However, it is a sad fact that, despite the effort and commitment and the money invested in diet literature and diet regimes, these attempts are rarely successful. Moreover, there is good evi-dence that – as we saw in Section 1 and again in Section 3 – dieting places people under physiological and psychological pressures to eat and, paradoxically, causes overeating.

For the great majority of people with bulimia nervosa, binge-eating began after they had started dieting. And for all of them, it is dieting that keeps the binge-eating going. In order to overcome bulimia nervosa and be confident of being able to eat 'normally', *you are going to have to give up the idea of dieting*.

Of course, this is a terrible prospect for someone who has dieted for years and who is terrified that if they stop dieting they will inevitably become fat. But if you are read-ing this book in the hope that it might help you deal with your eating problems, it is a simple truth that dieting has not worked: you are almost certainly heavier than you want to be and, despite wanting to lose weight, you periodically lose control and binge, which is guaranteed to prevent you from losing weight.

If you are binge-eating and dieting, it is worth asking yourself:

Is the average number of calories you absorb in a typical week really less than it would be if you were not binge-eating and dieting but were, instead, eating ordinary regular meals?

It is very difficult for anyone whose eating habits have become seriously disorganized and disturbed to answer this question. However, the truth is that, whatever efforts one goes to in order to compensate for overeating, a large number of calories is absorbed from a binge; and, in fact, it is usual that people who replace a pattern of eating characterized by dieting and binge-eating with one involving regular meals do not gain weight. Some people actually lose weight. This is worth emphasizing:

It is very rare that normal eating leads to significant weight gain.

Having read the previous section, you may well be thinking: 'Well, if I am not allowed to diet, this programme is not for me.' This is an understandable response; but the key point must be repeated in the strongest terms:

Dieting has not worked for you and it is a major factor causing you to binge.

You may well reply that, while it is true that dieting has failed in the sense that your eating habits are disorganized and out of control, it is, nevertheless, the case that if you were not dieting you would be even worse off since you would be eating far too much and would be gaining weight and in no time would be fat. This is a very strong conviction and a very compelling fear for many people with bulimia nervosa. However, the conviction is almost certainly wrong and the fear is almost certainly unfounded.

The truth is that for most people the replacement of a pattern of dieting and binge-eating with 'normal' meals does not have a significant effect on their weight.

It will be very difficult for anyone who has these convictions and fears to accept this statement on faith. The only way forward is to try the following experiment:

- For a four-week trial period, commit yourself to sticking to all the principles spelled out in this self-help course.

- After the four weeks, assess whether there has been an improvement in your eating habits and see what has happened to your weight.

The results of this experiment will help you decide whether it is worth continuing with the programme.

Vomiting and taking laxatives: the truth about 'compensating'

Vomiting encourages overeating. It is very common for people to say that when they first discovered vomiting as a method of dealing with overeating they felt elated. Suddenly they could eat what they wanted without it affecting their weight. However, they soon discovered that, far from liberating them, vomiting is a trap: vomiting leads to more eating, which in turn leads to more vomiting. Thus a vicious cycle is established where vomiting comes, in part, to encourage binge-eating.

Indeed, many people with bulimia nervosa find that, if they know that something is going to happen that will mean they can't vomit (for example, if they are going on a long car journey with friends), this acts as a temporary constraint on their eating. The implication for someone who wants to restore their eating habits to normal is that stopping vomiting will encourage them to exert more control over their eating.

In practice, of course, it is not as simple as this, and giving up vomiting as a method of escaping the consequences of overeating is far from easy. To some extent the same argument applies to the use of laxatives. Part Two of the programme will give you some advice on how to approach the task of giving up your methods of 'compensating' for overeating.

Depression

Depression often causes people with bulimia nervosa to binge. And binges make people depressed. Thus, another vicious cycle is set up.

Now, if you are making an effort not to binge then you are already attempting to break out of this cycle. However, many things other than overeating can make you feel depressed and thereby indirectly lead you to binge.

The implication here is that it is important for you to examine which aspects of your life are unsatisfactory and cause you to feel depressed, and to attempt to find solutions to these difficulties. You may well find the advice on problem-solving in Part Three of the course particularly helpful. It would also be a good idea to read Paul Gilbert's book *Overcoming Depression* (for details see the section of 'Useful Information' at the back of Part Three).

Do you require more help, perhaps with other problems?

The guidelines spelled out in Parts Two and Three of this course are essentially practical. They take problems with eating at face value: that is, they start from the fact that there are people who are distressed by being unable to control their eating and who want help in restoring their eating habits to normal. The manual is intended to provide these people with the tools they need to recover.

The guidelines are not, therefore, intended to help you uncover any deep reasons that might have caused your eating to become disordered in the first place. The reason for this is simply that the process of uncovering hidden causes is not necessary for restoring eating habits to 'normal'. That is to say, *it is perfectly possible for someone with bulimia nervosa to overcome her problems with eating simply by focusing on changing her eating habits and her attitudes towards weight and shape*. Given that this is possible, it seems sensible to specify how someone might achieve this end on her own.

Of course, some people may feel that the problems they have, including their eating disorder, arise directly from aspects of their early experience in ways they want to understand better, and they may well feel that a course of psychotherapy would be helpful to them in seeking this understanding. Similarly, some people may feel that a course of counselling would help them to deal with the day-to-day stresses of their lives.

Following the guidelines set out in this manual is not at odds with either of these options. Psychotherapy and counselling do not conflict with your dealing with your eating problems yourself; and you may feel that they would actually help you manage better with the self-help programme.

However, it must be emphasized that while these other treatments may or may not be helpful to you, for most people it is perfectly reasonable to expect that you will be able to restore order to your eating habits without such additional help.

Is now the right time to tackle your eating problems?

It is worth considering, before going any further with this manual, whether now is the right time for you to be tackling this problem. If you are going on holiday in two weeks, say, or you are studying for exams, you will not be able to devote yourself properly to the guidelines outlined in Parts Two and Three. In such circumstances, it would be best if you postponed beginning the programme until the time is right and you can make the necessary commitment. If you make a half-hearted start and then run into difficulties you may well become disheartened and give up on something that might work for you under the right circumstances.

On the other hand, unless there is a serious reason for not starting with this programme now – something as definite and important as a booked holiday or an exam

– you should commit yourself to beginning at a definite time in the near future. There will always be trivial reasons for putting off starting, and you should be suspicious of weak excuses!

Is there anything important going on, or about to happen, in your life, that makes this a bad time to start on the self-help programme? If so, write it in here:

_____

_____

_____

_____

_____

Now write down a date when this activity/demand will be over and when you can commit yourself fully to starting the programme:

_____

If there is no such important obstacle – pick up Part Two and prepare to start now!

Thoughts and Reflections

Thoughts and Reflections

Thoughts and Reflections

Thoughts and Reflections

Thoughts and Reflections

Thoughts and Reflections